ATLAN THE ARAKNE

The story begins with a young bread seller named Atlan, who carries a basket full of bread on his bicycle. He is handing out the bread to his regular customers, while greeting them with a smile.

The narrator says: "This is Atlan, a humble and hardworking bread seller. His life is simple, but happy."

Atlan arrives at a bakery, where his uncle Benito, who is the owner and the one who taught him the trade, is waiting for him.

Atlan gives him the money from the sales and tells him that he is going to school. Atlan tells him that he is proud of him and that he should continue studying.

The narrator says: "Atlan has a dream: to be a great scientist. That's why, after working, he goes to night school, where he learns everything he can."

Atlan enters the school, where he meets his friends and his girlfriend Ana.

Everyone welcomes him with joy and asks him how work went. Atlan tells them some funny anecdotes and tells them that he wants to learn.

The narrator says: "Atlan has a big heart and a good sense of humor. "His friends love him very much and support him in his goals."

Atlan attends a biology class, where the teacher talks to them about spiders and their characteristics.

Atlan is very interested and asks the teacher several questions.

The professor congratulates him for his curiosity and tells him that there is an exhibition about spiders in the museum of natural sciences.

The narrator says: "Peter has a passion for spiders. She is fascinated by his abilities and the diversity of him. Therefore, he decides to go to the museum the next day, to see the exhibition."

Atlan arrives at the museum, where there is a large billboard advertising the spider exhibition. Atlan enters excitedly and heads to the section where there are several terrariums with different species of live spiders. Atlan carefully observes each one of them and reads the information labels...

Atlan stops in front of a terrarium containing a very rare and exotic spider. The label says that it is a baker spider that lived in a cave, between the highest mountains; at very high depth, which was brought by a laboratory (3 steps away) to study its effects.

Atlan is impressed and moves closer to see her better.

The narrator says: "Atlan doesn't know it, but that spider is about to change his life forever."

The enormous spider, which feels threatened by Atlan's presence, jumps out of the terrarium and bites his hand. Atlan feels a sharp pain and walks away scared.

The spider falls to the ground and is seen by another visitor, who notices that it escapes through another door. Atlan looks at his hand and sees a big red mark.

The narrator says: "Atlan has been bitten by the spider. He bathes in blood; it mixes with the spider's venom, causing an unexpected reaction."

Atlan feels dizzy and leaves the museum. He gets on his bike and tries to return home. But along the way, she begins to notice some changes in her body. Her eyesight sharpens, his hearing amplifies, his strength increases and his balance improves.

Atlan arrives home, where his uncle Benito is waiting for him, who sees him pale and sweaty, bloody.

Benito asks him what's wrong and takes his temperature. Pedro tells him that he feels bad and that he was bitten by a spider in the museum.

Benito tells him that he should go to the doctor, but Atlan, despite his obvious image, tells him that it is not necessary and that he just needs to rest.

The narrator says: "Atlan doesn't want to worry his uncle anymore, but he doesn't know what's happening to him either. "His body is adapting to the changes caused by the spider's venom."

Atlan lies down on his bed and falls asleep. While he sleeps, he has a strange dream, where he sees himself climbing walls, shooting cobwebs and swinging off buildings.

He also sees various criminals assaulting, robbing and killing people. Atlan feels a strong responsibility to stop them and use his powers for good.

The narrator says: "Atlan, dying, is experiencing a vision of his future. A memory of the future where he is a hero who fights evil with his spider powers."

Atlan wakes up the next day, feeling better and more energetic.

He gets out of bed and looks in the mirror. She is surprised to see that her body has changed:

He is more muscular, taller and more handsome.

He also notices that his eyes are brighter and that he has small bumps on his forearms.

The narrator says: "Atlan has completed his immunity. "He now has the abilities of a spider, such as strength, agility, spider sense and the ability to generate webs on his own."

Atlan decides to test his new powers and leaves his house. He heads to a tall building and starts climbing the wall. He then jumps into the void and launches a vine of spider tissue for the first time.
Atlan swings through the air, feeling great excitement and freedom, as he enjoys his new condition. However, he does not realize that he is being watched by a mysterious man, who recognizes him as the bread seller who visited the museum.

The man...

Atlan realizes that he has a spider sense that alerts him to dangers.

When a bully tries to hit him, Atlan easily dodges him and makes a fool of him. Or when a girl approaches him with the intention of robbing him, Atlan discovers her and rejects her.

The narrator says: "Atlan has an advantage over the others. His spider sense allows him to anticipate situations and react quickly. But it also makes him feel different and isolated."

Atlan leaves school and heads to work.
On the way, he sees a robbery at a jewelry store. Atlan without hiding his person, he decides to use his powers to stop the thieves.

Atlan goes into action and surprises the thieves with his webs and blows. Atlan manages to capture the thieves and leaves them tied up for the police.
The narrator says: "Atlan has made a decision. He has decided to use his powers to help others and fight crime. A new hero has been born...

Atlan arrives at his uncle and aunt's bakery, where he works as a bread deliveryman.

His uncle congratulates him for his good work and gives him a tip. His aunt asks him how he did in school and if he has a girlfriend.

Atlan tells them that everything is fine and that he has no time for love. Atlan feels happy to have a family that loves and supports him.

The narrator says: "Atlan has a normal and simple life. But he also has a secret. "He is a defender of justice."

Atlan returns to the museum where he gained his powers.

He wants to know more about spiders and their origin.

Atlan enters the museum and heads to the arachnology section. There he sees an exhibition of different species of spiders, their habitats, their behaviors and their characteristics. Atlan is fascinated by the world of spiders and tries to learn everything he can.

The narrator says: "Atlan seeks answers to his questions. "He wants to understand how he became Spider-Man and what responsibility comes with having his powers."

Atlan finds a display case showing the spider that bit him.

The spider is indigo in color, with a geometric pattern on its abdomen. Atlan reads the information that comes with the spider.

He says that it is a genetically unknown spider, found by a group of scientists to study the effects of its venom on living beings.

The spider escaped from the lab during a school trip and bit a student, who turned out to be Atlan.

The narrator says: "Atlan discovers the truth about his origin. He is the result of a scientific experiment that went wrong, they were trying to test this poison on living beings and verify its lethality.

"He is the only human being who survived the spider's venom."

But scientists still don't know, and they consider that student dead, since the incident was only slightly captured...
Atlan uses his powers in the museum to explore the different rooms and exhibits.

Atlan climbs walls, jumps across ceilings, swings through cobwebs, and slides across floors.

Atlan has fun and feels free. The narrator says: "Atlan enjoys his powers. He can do things that no one else can. He feels special and unique."

Atlan catches the attention of the museum guards, who see him as an intruder and a threat.

The guards try to capture Atlan, but he evades them with his agility and cunning. Pedro makes jokes and humiliates them.

Atlan mocks the guards and challenges them. The narrator says: "Atlan trusts in his powers.

He believes he can do whatever he wants without consequences. "He feels superior and irresponsible."

Atlan meets a group of students who also visited the museum the day he was bitten by the spider.

Among them is María, a girl with whom Atlan is in love.
Atlan approaches María and tries to impress her with his powers. Atlan tells him that he has powers and that he can do incredible things.

Atlan shows him his webs and his strength.

The narrator says: "Atlan wants to get María's attention. He believes that her powers are an advantage to conquer her. He feels confident and romantic."

María is scared when she sees Atlan's powers.

She thinks Atlan is a monster and a freak.

She tells Atlan to stay away from her and not bother her again.

She yells at the other students that Atlan is Spider-Man and that he is dangerous. The students get scared and run away from the museum.

Atlan is left alone and sad.

The narrator says: "Atlan makes a mistake when he reveals his identity to María. He doesn't know that his powers can cause fear and rejection. He feels disappointed and lonely."

Atlan learns to hide his personal identity, developing a new one.
He makes a suit of red and blue cloth, with a mask that covers his face.

He also makes 3-fingered gloves that allow him to look less human, giving a more intimidating appearance at night, and providing better grip on surfaces.

He keeps his suit in his backpack and uses it when he needs to act like a hero.

The narrator says: "Atlan has created his secret identity.

He calls himself, like in some comics and movies he's seen.

He is dedicated to protecting the city from criminals and villains.

"He feels proud and heroic."

Some time later we can see him, in the city with a halfway decent suit, living with a new way of seeing the world...

A naive boy named Atlan swings across the city buildings with a spider web.

He wears a red and blue suit with a mask covering his face.
He has a more acute spider sense that alerts him to dangers.

Atlan sees some robbers leaving a bank with bags of money. He lunges towards them and catches them with his web.

The robbers fire their weapons, but Atlan dodges the bullets with his agility and reflexes.

Atlan turns the thieves over to the police and tells them that he gave them to them as a gift.

The police thank him and tell him he is a hero. Atlan smiles and leaves.

Atlan arrives home and takes off his suit.

He looks in the mirror and tells himself that he is a normal boy with a normal life, except for his spider powers.

He wonders if one day he will be able to reveal his secret to the girl he likes, María...

Atlan receives a call from his uncle Ben, who tells him that he is waiting for him at the cinema to watch a movie.

Atlan tells him that he's coming and puts his suit back on.

He says goodbye to his aunt Mari, who tells him to be careful.

Atlan climbs out the window and swings through the city, thinking about what awaits him.

Atlan arrives at the cinema and meets his uncle Ben, who hugs him and tells him that he has bought tickets to see the new Spider-Man movie.

Atlan is surprised and wonders if his uncle knows anything about his secret identity.

He tells him that he loves Spider-Man and that he is his favorite hero.

Atlan and his uncle Benito enter the movie theater and sit in their seats.

Atlan sees that María is sitting a few rows ahead.

Atlan feels a knot in his stomach and gets nervous.

His Uncle Ben tells him not to worry, there are plenty of fish in the sea.

The movie begins and Pedro is hypnotized by Spider-Man's action scenes.

He identifies with the character and imagines that he is the one fighting villains and saving people.
Suddenly, his phone rings and he sees that it's a police alert. There is a robbery at a bank near the cinema.

Atlan tells his uncle Ben that he has to go to the bathroom and runs out of the room.

He buys a spiderman cosplay, under his clothes, and looks for a way out.

He sees an open window and jumps through it. He shoots a web and swings towards the bank, hoping to arrive in time to stop the robbers.

Atlan arrives at the bank and sees that the robbers are armed and have hostages.

One of them has a spiderman mask and a leather jacket with Skull's name on the back.

Atlan recognizes the leader of the band, it is Jorge, María's boyfriend. Atlan stands paralyzed for a moment, not knowing what to do.

Atlan decides to act and attacks the thieves.

It shoots webs at them and immobilizes them. The hostages take the opportunity to escape and call the police.

Atlan confronts Jorge, who points a gun at him.

Jorge tells him that he knows who he is and that he is going to destroy him.

Atlan is surprised and asks how he knows.

Jorge tells him that he recognized him by his voice and the way he moved.

She tells him that she has been following him since she saw him with Maria at the movies.

He tells her that María is his and that no one is going to take her away from him.

Atlan gets angry and tells her that María belongs to no one, that she is a free person and that she can choose who to be with.

He tells her that he respects her and loves her, but that he has never said anything to her for fear of losing her friendship.

She tells him that Jorge doesn't deserve her, that he is a criminal and an abuser.

Jorge laughs and tells him that Atlan is a loser, a coward.

He tells him that he is the best, the strongest and the most handsome.

He tells him that María loves him and will never leave him.

He tells him that he is the real Spider-Man, the city's hero, and if he didn't become the...

Atlan is outraged and tells him that he is not SpiderMan, that he is just an imposter who uses a mask to hide his evil.

He tells him that he is not one either, but he would be a hero, the one who fights for justice and peace.

He tells him that he is the one who is going to arrest him and take him to jail.

Jorge shoots Atlan, but he dodges the bullet with his spider sense.

Atlan throws a web at the gun and takes it out of his hands.

Jorge becomes enraged and throws himself at Atlan, trying to hit him with his fists.

Atlan and Jorge get into a hand-to-hand fight.

Atlan uses his agility and strength to dodge and counterattack Jorge's blows.

Jorge uses his experience and cunning to surprise and hurt Atlan.

The two hurt each other, but neither gives up.

The police arrive at the bank and surround the place.
The agents see the fight between Atlan and Jorge and don't know who is the good guy and who is the bad guy.

One of them recognizes Jorge as the leader of the Skull gang and tells the others to shoot the one wearing the Spiderman mask, but with the gang's jacket.

The police shoot Jorge, but Atlan gets in the way and takes the bullets to his body.

Atlan falls to the ground, bleeding and dying.

Jorge takes advantage of the situation and takes off Atlan's Spider-Man cosplay, leaving him in his underwear. Jorge puts on the Spider-Man cosplay and pretends to be him.

Jorge approaches the police and tells them that he is Spider-Man, that he has stopped the thieves and that he has saved the hostages.

He tells them that the one on the ground is Skull, the villain who wanted to rob the bank.

He tells them to arrest him and take him to jail.

The police believe Jorge and congratulate him for his heroism.

They tell him that he is an example for the city and that they are going to give him a medal. They ask him if he needs anything and he tells them yes, he wants to see María, his girlfriend.

The police call María and tell her to come to the bank, that there is a surprise for her.

María gets scared and thinks that something has happened to her...

He gets in a taxi and goes to the bank as fast as he can.

María arrives at the bank and sees Jorge dressed as Spider-Man, surrounded by police and journalists.

Jorge sees her and hugs her, telling her that he loves her and that he has done everything for her.

María is confused and does not understand anything.

María sees Pedro lying on the floor, in his underwear, bleeding.

María is horrified and lets go of Jorge.

He runs to Atlan and hugs him, crying uncontrollably.

He tells him he's sorry, that he loves him, not to leave him.

Atlan opens his eyes and sees María. She smiles weakly at him and tells him that he loves her too, that he has always loved her. Other neighbors see the scene, including Ana, Atlan's ex-girlfriend...

He tells Maria that he is the one who has saved the city on some occasions, that he is the one who has the spider powers, who tried to be Spider-Man.

He tells him that Jorge is an imposter, a thief and a murderer.

He tells him to tell the police the truth and they will arrest him.

María remains paralyzed, unable to believe what Atlan tells her.

He asks him how it is possible, how he got his powers, how Jorge is an imposter...

Atlan, still wounded, tells him that there is no time for explanations, so he has to act quickly before Jorge escapes or kills him.

Jorge realizes that Atlan is alive and becomes angry.

He lets go of María and throws himself at Jorge, ready to end this.

Atlan reacts and uses his webs to tie Jorge and throw him against a wall.

The police officers get confused, Maria points at Jorge then they take advantage of the opportunity and shoot him with stun guns, leaving him unconscious.

Atlan gets up with difficulty and approaches María.

He tells her that he loves her, that he has always loved her, that she forgive him for hiding his identity from her.

Maria hugs him and tells him that she loves him too, that she doesn't care who he is, that she just wants to be with him.

The journalists approach and ask them questions, wanting to know the truth about Spider-Man.

Atlan tells them that he is not Spider-Man, that this is just a cosplay, that Jorge is a fake who stole his costume.

He tells them that he is a hero, who fights for justice and peace.

The police confirm Atlan's version and arrest Jorge.

They take off his suit and discover that he is an average man, a former self-service employee, who went crazy, and was a gang leader.

They nickname him "Skull" and take him to an ordinary prison.

Atlan and Maria kiss passionately, while journalists take photos of them and applaud them.

Ana disappears from the scene...

Atlan tells María that he has to leave, that he has a mission to fulfill, that he has to protect the city from other villains, and that he also has to heal his wounds.

María tells him to wait for him, not to leave, to stay with her.

Atlan tells her that he loves her, but that he has a responsibility, that he has great power and a great duty.

He tells him that he will not be Spider-Man, but "Arakne", the friend of the people...

Shortly after, Atlan faces a peculiar enemy: the subject has extra robotic joints on his back, in the form of additional prostheses...

The narrator says: "Atlan has a new challenge.

He must face a modern enemy, a villain who is stronger than the rest. He must use his powers and his wits to defeat him."

It also marks the beginning of a competition between, natural evolution, against technology and ingenuity...

Atlan launched himself from the roof of a building, swinging his webs towards the center of the city.
She had received an emergency call from her friend and teammate, Lila, who had been captured by Modem, the leader of a criminal organization that used technology for its evil purposes.

Modem called himself that because he could control any electronic device with his mind, thanks to a cybernetic implant that had been placed in his brain.

He was a hacking and computer genius, and had an obsession with proving his superiority over heroes who used their natural abilities.

Atlan knew that Modem was a dangerous enemy, and that he had to rescue Lila before it was too late.

Lila was a mutant with the power to manipulate sound, and could create devastating sonic waves with her voice. Together they were a formidable team, but apart they were vulnerable.

Atlan arrived at the place where Modem had summoned Lila, an old abandoned factory full of machinery and cables. He entered cautiously, looking for any sign of his friend or his enemy. Suddenly, he heard a malicious laugh echo through the speakers.

- Welcome, Atlan - said Modem's voice -. I'm glad you have come. This way I can show you how useless your power is compared to mine.

- Where is Lila? - Atlan asked, furious -. What have you done to him?

- Don't worry about her - Modem replied -. She's fine, for now. I have her tied to a chair in the control room.

- But I don't think he'll really like what I'm going to do with you.

- What do you mean? - Atlan asked, confused.

- You see, I have prepared a little game for you - Modem explained -.

- I have connected this factory to my brain, and I can turn any machine on or off just by thinking about it. Your mission is to get to the control room and free Lila. But it won't be easy. Along the way you will have to face my death traps, designed especially for you.

- Death traps? - Atlan repeated, incredulous -. What kind of crazy are you?

- "I'm a madman with a purpose," Modem said. I want to show the world that technology is superior to natural evolution. That I am superior to you. And for that I need to eliminate you.

- "You won't make it," Atlan said, determined. I will not give in to you. I'm going to save you Lila and stop you.

- That remains to be seen - said Modem -. The game starts now. Good luck, Atlan. You're going to need it.

And then the communication was cut off. Atlan looked around, trying to find his way to the control room.

He knew he had to be quick and cunning to avoid Modem's traps. But he also knew that he had something that Modem didn't: the courage of a hero.

Atlan moved through the factory, dodging the machines that turned on and off at random.

He could feel Modem's presence in his mind, taunting him and daring him to continue.

Atlan ignored him, and concentrated on his objective: to reach Lila and free her.

He used his spider senses to detect danger and his reflexes to react.

He jumped onto a fast-moving conveyor belt, ducked under a forcefully lowering hydraulic press, swung over an abyss filled with electrified cables. It wasn't easy, but it wasn't impossible either.

- Is that all you have, Modem? - thought Atlan -. You're going to have to try harder if you want to stop me.

But Modem did not give up. On the contrary, he increased the difficulty of his traps, and began using his power to interfere with the electronic devices Atlan carried with him.

Your communicator, your locator, your watch. Everything stopped working.

- What's wrong with you, Atlan? - Modem said over the speakers -. Are you lost? Need help? Don't worry, I'll give it to you.
- You just have to follow the arrows that I have put for you.

Atlan looked around, and saw red arrows pointing in a direction.

He didn't pay attention to them, and decided to go the other way.

- Bad choice, Atlan - said Modem -. You have fallen into my trap.

Suddenly, a door closed behind him, and another in front. He was trapped in a room with no way out.

He looked around, and saw that the walls were covered in screens. Images of Lila were projected on them, tied to a chair and with electrodes in her head.

- Lilac! - Atlan exclaimed -. Leave her alone!

- "I'm sorry, Atlan," Modem said. But this is part of the game. You see, I've hooked up Lila's brain to a sonic wave generator. Every time she thinks about something, the generator makes a sound that causes her pain. And the louder the sound, the more pain it causes you.

- You are a monster - said Atlan -. What do you want from her?

- "I want you to help me finish you off," Modem said. I want him to use his power to create a sonic wave so powerful it will destroy your eardrums. And for that I need him to think about you.

- "He won't," Atlan said. She loves me. And I her.

- "That's what you think," Modem said. But maybe I'll change my mind when I see this.

Then the screens changed images, and showed scenes from Atlan's past. Scenes in which he had lied, betrayed or hurt other people. Scenes that he preferred to forget.

- **What is this? - Atlan asked -. How do you know all this?**

- **"I know everything about you, Atlan," Modem said. I've hacked into your medical history, your school records, your social profile. I have analyzed your tastes, your fears, your secrets. I have created a complete psychological profile of you. And I discovered something interesting: you have a guilt complex.**

- **A complex of what? - Atlan asked.**
- **Of guilt - Modem repeated -. You feel guilt for everything you have done wrong in your life.**

- **For being bitten by a spider and gaining your powers. For having abandoned your girlfriend Ana, for not being able to combine your life as a hero and as a civilian. For having failed your friends, your family, your city.**

- **It's not true - said Atlan -. I don't feel guilty about any of that.**

- Of course yes - Modem insisted -. And I'm going to use that guilt to make you suffer. I'm going to make Lila watch all those scenes, and let her know what you really are: a liar, a traitor, a failure. And when she knows it, she will hate you. And she will use her power to kill you.

- "He won't do it," Atlan repeated. She knows me. She knows I'm good.

- Sure? - asked Modem -. What if I tell you that there is something you haven't told him? Something that could change everything.

- What are you taking about? - Atlan asked, nervous.

- I'm talking about this - said Modem, and showed a new image on the screens.

Atlan gasped when he saw her. It was a photo of him kissing another girl. A girl who wasn't Lila.

- What is this? - Atlan asked, confused.

- **This is proof of your infidelity - said Modem -. This is what you did two weeks ago, when you went to a party with your friends. You got drunk, and you hooked up with this girl.**

- **You don't remember his name, but I do. Her name is Maria, and she is the girlfriend of your ex-friend Jorge... Now Skull.**

- **It can't be - said Atlan -. I didnot do that.**

- **Yes you did - said Modem -. And I have the video to prove it.**

Then the screens showed a video in which Atlan and Maria were seen kissing passionately on a sofa.

Atlan couldn't believe what he saw. He didn't remember anything from that night. But the images were clear.

- **This is a setup - said Atlan -. You have manipulated the images.**

- **"No, I haven't," Modem said. This is real. And Lila is going to see it. And when she sees it, she will feel betrayed. And she will hate you. And she will kill you.**

- No, please - Atlan begged -. Don't do that to him. Don't show him that. She doesn't deserve it.

- "I'm sorry, Atlan," Modem said. But the game is over. The moment of the truth has come. Goodbye, Atlan.

And then the screens went off, and there was silence.
Atlan felt a chill run through his body. He knew that he was in a desperate situation. Not only was he trapped in a dead-end room, but he was also about to lose the person he loved most in the world.

- Lila, please don't hate me - Atlan thought.

- . I love you. I would never hurt you.

But his thoughts did not reach Lila. She could only see the images that Modem showed her on the screens. Images of Atlan kissing another girl. Images that broke his heart.

- How could you, Atlan? - thought Lila -.

- How could you fool me like that? Don't you love me? Don't you care about me?

Lila felt a mixture of pain, anger and sadness.

I wanted to cry, scream, escape. But she couldn't.

She was tied to a chair, and connected to a sonic wave generator.

Every time he thought about something, the generator made a sound that caused him pain. And the louder the sound, the more pain it caused him.

- This is what you deserve, Atlan - Modem said over the speakers -. This is what happens when you betray someone who loves you. Now you are going to pay for your mistake. Now you are going to die.

Modem increased the intensity of the generator, and the sound became higher pitched and louder. Lila felt an unbearable pain in her head, and she couldn't help but scream.

- Aaaah! - Lila shouted -. For! For!

His scream turned into a sonic wave that shot towards the room where Atlan was. The sonic wave was so powerful that it passed through walls and glass, and reached Atlan's ears.

Atlan heard Lila's scream, and knew it was her. He knew that she was suffering because of her. He knew that she was using her power to kill him.

- No, Lila! - Atlan exclaimed -. Do not do it! I love you!

But his words did not reach Lila. She could only hear the sound of the generator, and the echo of her own scream. A scream that she repeated over and over again, each time louder and more lethal.

Atlan felt an unbearable pain in his ears, and he put his hands to his head. The sonic wave was destroying his eardrums, causing him to lose his balance and orientation.

- Aaaah! - Atlan shouted -. For! For!

But Lila didn't stop. She continued screaming, not controlling her power. She continued sending sonic waves towards Atlan, not knowing what she was doing.

Modem watched the scene with satisfaction.

He had achieved his goal: to make Lila kill Atlan with her own power.

He had demonstrated his superiority over them.

- **I've done it - Modem thought -. I have won the game.**

But then something happened, something Modem didn't expect. Something that changed the course of events.

Atlan felt the pain of the sonic waves piercing his body. He knew he couldn't hold out much longer.

But he couldn't give up either. He had to save Lila, his partner, his friend, his love.

With one last effort, he launched himself towards Modem, ready to risk everything.

Modem was surprised to see him coming.

I didn't expect him to have such a will to live.

- **Impossible! - Modem exclaimed -. You can not beat me!**

But Atlan didn't pay attention to him. He used his spider powers to shoot a web that covered Modem's face, momentarily blinding him.

Then, he took advantage of the distraction to hit him hard in the chest, making him fall to the ground.

Atlan approached Lila, who was still tied to the chair and screaming. She removed the neural connections caused by her pain and covered his mouth with her hand.

- Lila, it's me, Atlan - he whispered in her ear -.

- You are safe. It won't hurt you anymore.

Lila opened her eyes and recognized Atlan. A tear of relief rolled down her cheek.

- Atlan... - Lila murmured -. Thank you...

Atlan hugged her tenderly and untied her from the chair. Then, he picked her up in his arms and ran out of the place, leaving behind Modem, who stood up furious.

- They won't escape! - Modem shouted -. I will find them and destroy them!

But Atlan and Lila were no longer listening to him. They only had each other. And that was all they needed.

Atlan and Lila managed to escape Modem's clutches, but they knew they couldn't let their guard down.

Modem was a powerful and ruthless enemy, who would stop at nothing to capture them and use them for his evil plans.

- **What does Modem want from us? - Lila asked, as they took refuge in an abandoned house.**

- **I don't know - Atlan responded -. But it has something to do with our powers. I think he wants to extract them and use them to create an ultimate weapon.**

- **An ultimate weapon? - Lila repeated, scared -. So that?**

- **I don't know - Atlan admitted -. But we can't let him do it. We have to stop it.**

- **As? - Lila inquired -. We have no idea where its base is or how to get into it.**

- **"Maybe we can find out," Atlan suggested. Remember that Modem has a mental connection with us. Maybe we can use it to our advantage.**

- **As? - Lila insisted -. Won't it be dangerous?**

- Maybe - Atlan acknowledged -. But it's our only option. We have to try.

Atlan took Lila's hand and looked into her eyes.

- Trust me - he said -. Together we can do it.

Lila nodded and looked back at him.

- Okay I accept -. I trust you.

Atlan and Lila closed their eyes and concentrated. They attempted to establish a mental connection with Modem, using his spider and sonic powers. At first, they didn't feel anything. But then, they began to perceive a dark and malevolent presence in their minds.

It was Modem...

Atlan and Lila managed to enter Modem's mind, but what they saw there horrified them.

Modem had a distorted view of reality, where he believed himself to be the master of the world and others were his slaves.

Its base was a huge underground laboratory, full of macabre machines and experiments.

There, Modem extracted the powers of other beings like them, and combined them to create an ultimate weapon: a sonic bomb capable of destroying anything that stood in its path.

- "This is crazy," Lila said, trembling. We have to get out of here.

- We can't - said Atlan -. We have to stop it. We have to find a way to defuse the bomb.

- As? - Lila asked -. We know nothing about bombs or technology.

- Maybe we can use our powers - Atlan proposed -. Maybe we can interfere with the bomb's sonic frequency and make it explode before it drops it.

- What if he discovers us? - Lila questioned -. What if she attacks us with her mind?

- "Then we will have to fight," Atlan replied. But we have no choice. It's our only hope.

Atlan and Lila gathered their courage and headed towards the center of the laboratory, where the bomb was. Modem was there, proudly watching over his creation.

- **What do we have here? - said Modem, noticing his presence -. Two mice that have sneaked into my mind? How curious. What do they seek? What do they want?**

- **"We want you to stop," Atlan said firmly. We want you to stop hurting others. We want you to leave us alone.**

- **How naive - Modem mocked -. They don't know who they're messing with. They don't know what I'm capable of doing. They do not know what awaits them.**

Modem launched a mental attack against Atlan and Lila, attempting to bend them to his will.

But Atlan and Lila resisted, using their spider and sonic powers to counter the attack.

- **They won't be able to beat me - said Modem -. I am stronger than you. I'm smarter than you. I am more powerful than you.**
- **"You're not," said Lila. You are a monster. You are a tyrant. You are crazy.**

- **"Don't insult me," Modem said. You will regret me.**

Modem increased the intensity of his mental attack, causing Atlan and Lila to feel unbearable pain.

- Aaaah! - Atlan and Lila shouted, in unison.

But they didn't give up. They knew they had to move on. They knew they had to save the world.

The fight between Atlan, Lila and Modem developed in a dramatic and epic way.

Atlan and Lila used their spider and sonic powers to resist Modem's mental attack, as they approached the bomb.

Modem tried to stop them with everything he had, but he couldn't stop them from reaching the device.

- Don't do it! - Modem warned them -. If they touch the bomb, they will explode it!

- "That's what we want," Atlan said. We want to end your madness.

- They are crazy! - said Modem -. They do not know what they do!

Atlan and Lila ignored his words and put their hands on the bomb. They attempted to alter the sonic frequency of the bomb with their powers, to make it detonate prematurely. The bomb began to vibrate and make a high-pitched sound.

- We did it! - Lila exclaimed -. The bomb is going to explode!

- We have to get out of here! - said Atlan -. We have to get back to our bodies!

Atlan and Lila let go of the bomb and walked away from it. They tried to get out of Modem's mind, but ran into a problem.

- I cant go out! - Lila said -. Modem has blocked our exit!

- That! - said Atlan -. That is not possible!

- It is! - said Modem, with an evil laugh -. I've trapped them in my mind! They won't be able to escape! They will die with me!

Modem had used his last resort: he had closed his mind, preventing Atlan and Lila from leaving it. She had decided to take her enemies with him to the grave.

- It just can't be! - said Atlan -. Can not do that!

- It has done! - Lila said -. We are doomed!

- "No, we are not," Atlan said. There is still hope.

- Which? - Lila asked.

- Our love - Atlan responded.

Atlan hugged Lila and kissed her passionately. She transmitted to him all her love, all her strength, all her trust. Lila returned the same sentiment. They merged into one being, one soul.

And then a miracle happened.

Their love was so powerful, so pure, so true, that it broke the barriers of Modem's mind. She created a gap through which they could get out. They broke free from their mental prison and returned to their bodies.
Just in time.

The bomb exploded in Modem's laboratory, causing a huge explosion that destroyed everything. Modem died instantly, unable to believe what had happened.

Atlan and Lila woke up in the abandoned house where they had taken refuge. They looked into each other's eyes and smiled. They were alive. They were together. They had saved the world.

Time after:

Parasites are entities that take over a person's body, turning them into their host.

Despite the name, Parasites are not completely harmful, as they create nutrients for the host's body in exchange for improving its combat capabilities. For example, some Parasites can grant the host superhuman strength, speed, or endurance.

However, not all Parasites are the same. Some can separate and become independent from the host, and act of their own will. These are classified as Remote Parasites, and are usually more dangerous and aggressive than the others.

In the past, the Parasites were known as Theons, and their hosts as Avatars.

The Theons / Terrones were venerated as divine beings.

Until some, caused the world to fear such beings, leading to the discrimination that many face today."...

Atlan and Lila had managed to escape from the villains' secret base, where they had been captured and tortured.

Atlan used his spider powers to climb the walls and free Lila from her cell. Lila used her sonic vocal powers to break the doors and stun the guards. Together, they ran towards the exit, but ran into the leader of the villains, a man named ContraFace.
Contraface was a former friend of Atlan, who had been infected by a parasite that gave him superhuman strength, speed, and endurance, but also made him crazy and evil.

Contraface wanted to use the parasite to create an army of invincible soldiers, and that is why he had kidnapped Atlan and Lila, to study their powers and replicate them.

- Counterface: Atlan, my old friend! What are you doing running away with this girl? Don't you know that she is a threat to our plan? You should join me! Together we could dominate the world with our powers.

- **Atlan: No, Counterface! You are not my friend. You are a monster who has lost his humanity. Lila is my partner, and I'm not going to let you hurt her. Let's stop you!**

- **Lila: That's right, Counterface! You have nothing to offer us. You just want to use our powers for your selfish purposes. We are not afraid of you!**
- **Counterface: How naive you are! You can't face me. I am stronger, faster and more resistant than you. Also, I have something that you don't have: the parasite. Look what it can do!**

Contraface activated his parasite, which covered his body in a slimy substance, giving him the appearance of a giant spider. Her eyes turned white and her teeth became sharp. Her hands turned into claws and her mouth into a jaw full of fangs.

- **Counterface: Now! The supreme predator! Nobody can stop me!**

- **Atlan: We're not afraid of you, Counterface! You're not the only one who can shapeshift! I can too!**

Atlan activated a type of improvised armor that allowed him to have an additional exoskeleton on his suit.

Atlan: Now I'm Atlan! The spider hero! I'm ready to fight!

- Lila: And me too! I won't be left behind! Lila activated her sonic vocal powers, allowing her to emit sound waves of high frequency and intensity. Her hair turned pink and her eyes green. Her lips lit up with a blue glow. Her voice became more powerful and melodious.

- Lila: Now I'm Lila! The Sonic Singer! I'm ready to sing!

The three launched into combat, starting an epic battle between good and evil.

Atlan used hooks on his suit to swing through the air and attack Contraface from different angles, with his natural webbing.

Lila used her voice to create shock waves that hit Contraface and made him flinch.

Counterface used his claws to try to catch Atlan and Lila, and his jaw to try to bite them.

The fight was intense and violent, with punches, screams and bites.

None of the three gave up, and none of the three managed to defeat the other. The battle seemed to have no end, until something unexpected happened.

Suddenly, the Contraface parasite began to react strangely.

It began to shake and change color, going from gray to red. Contraface felt unbearable pain, and began to scream.

- Counterface: Aaaah! What's happening to me! What is the parasite doing to me!

- Atlan: It's the sound! Lila's sound is affecting the parasite! It's her weakness!

- Lila: Then we have to take advantage! We have to increase the volume!

Lila concentrated all her energy into her voice, and began to sing a very high and very strong note.

The sound was so powerful that it made the entire place vibrate. The parasite could not bear it, and began to detach itself from Contraface's body, revealing the man underneath.

- **Counterface: No! Don't abandon me, parasite! Do not leave me alone!**

- **Atlan: It's our chance! We must put an end to it!**

Atlan launched himself at Contraface, and entangled him with his web, immobilizing him.

Contraface collapsed to the ground, unconscious. Atlan and Lila hugged each other, relieved and happy.

- **Atlan: We have done it! We have defeated Contraface!**

- **Lila: Yes! We have been a great team!**

- **Atlan: I love you, Lila!**

- **Lila: And I love you, Atlan!**

While the parasite crawled on the ground, looking for a new host...

There are many types of Parasites, each with its own characteristics and abilities. Some examples are:

- **Fire Parasites:** These are Parasites that can generate and manipulate fire. Their hosts can breathe flames, create heat shields, or become immune to fire. They are very powerful, but also very unstable and prone to anger.
- **Water Parasites:** They are Parasites that can control water and its states. Their hosts can create waves, freeze water, or breathe underwater. They are very versatile, but also very sensitive and emotional.

- **Air Parasites:** These are Parasites that can dominate the air and wind. Their hosts can fly, create tornadoes, or generate vacuum. They are very agile, but also very scattered and distracted.

- **Earth Parasites:** These are Parasites that can handle earth and minerals. Their hosts can lift rocks, create earthquakes, or harden their skin. They are very strong, but also very stubborn and stubborn.

- **Light Parasites:** These are Parasites that can emit and reflect light. Their hosts can illuminate, blind, or create illusions. They are very intelligent, but also very proud and arrogant.

- **Darkness Parasites:** These are Parasites that can absorb and project darkness. Their hosts can hide, scare, or create nightmares. They are very cunning, but also very cruel and evil.

These are just a few examples, but there are many more types of Parasites in the world. Each has its advantages and disadvantages, and it is up to the host how to use them for good or evil.

There are several ways to acquire a Parasite, but none are safe or guaranteed. Some of them are:

- **Being infected by a Remote Parasite:** Some Remote Parasites seek new hosts to expand their influence and power. They can attack a person and try to enter their body, either through the skin, blood or mouth. If the Parasite manages to fuse with the host, it will grant it its powers, but it will also impose its will and personality on it. This way of acquiring a Parasite is very dangerous, as it can result in the loss of the host's identity and sanity.

- **Being chosen by a Parasite: Some Parasites have criteria for selecting their hosts, based on their physical, mental or emotional characteristics. They can sense the presence of a person compatible with them, and try to communicate with them. If the person accepts the Parasite, a voluntary and harmonious union will occur, which will benefit both. This way of acquiring a Parasite is very rare, as it requires a special affinity between the Parasite and the host.**

- **Being exposed to a source of Parasites: Some sources of Parasites are places, objects or events that contain or generate Parasites. They can be natural or artificial, ancient or modern, known or secret. A person who approaches a Parasite source may be exposed to the source's influence, and receive a random Parasite.**

This way of acquiring a Parasite is very unpredictable, as it can result in a successful or unsuccessful union, depending on the compatibility between the Parasite and the host.

Atlan swung between the buildings of the city, enjoying the feeling of freedom that his spider powers gave him. He was a sixteen-year-old boy who had been bitten by a genetically modified spider in a secret laboratory. Since then, he had developed incredible abilities, such as strength, agility, spider sense, and the ability to shoot webs from his wrists.
Atlan considered himself a hero, and used his powers to help people and fight crime. However, not everyone saw it that way. Some feared him, others hated him and others wanted to capture him to study him. That's why Atlan wore a black mask with white eyes and a dark blue suit with red stripes when he went out on patrol.
One night, while heading home after stopping some thieves, Atlan felt a vibration in his spider sense. Something bad was happening nearby. He followed the trail until he reached an abandoned factory, where he saw a scene that left him frozen.
A man in a metallic moth suit was attacking another man in a black suit and a red hood. The Mothman called himself Lepidum, and he was a villain who used his suit to fly and shoot high-intensity red ions that could be deadly. The man in the hood called himself The Ninja, and he was an antihero who used his martial arts skills and hidden weapons to fight evil.

Atlan recognized El Ninja from the news. He was a vigilante who acted on his behalf, without caring about the laws or the consequences. He sometimes helped people, but other times he took justice into his own hands, killing or torturing his enemies. Atlan wasn't sure if he was an ally or an enemy. What he was sure of was that Lepidum was a danger to everyone, and that he had to stop him. Without a second thought, Atlan launched into combat, shooting webs at Lepidum to distract him.

- Hey, weirdo! Atlan shouted. Why don't you take on someone your size?

Lepidum turned angrily and saw Atlan hanging from a spider web.

- Who are you? -asked Lepidum-. Another annoying insect?
- "I'm not an insect, I'm a spider," Atlan corrected. And I'm here to stop you.
- Stop me? -Lepidum laughed-. With what? With your sticky threads?

Lepidum fired a beam of red ions at Atlan, but he dodged it with agility.

- "Not only do I have sticky threads," Atlan said. I also have this.

Atlan shot a web into Lepidum's face, momentarily blinding him. She then approached him and punched him in the chest, making him retreat.

- Ouch! -exclaimed Lepidum-. That hurt!

- "It will hurt you more if you don't give up," Atlan threatened. I don't want to hurt you, I just want you to stop hurting others.
- And who are you to tell me what to do? -replied Lepidum-. A boy with a hero complex?
- "I am more than that," Atlan stated. Am...

Before he could finish his sentence, a ninja star grazed his cheek, causing him to bleed.

- Careful! -The Ninja shouted from behind him-. This is my fight, don't get involved.

Atlan turned around in surprise and saw The Ninja with an angry expression.

- What are you doing? Atlan asked. Can't you see I'm trying to help you?
- "I don't need your help," The Ninja replied. This guy stole something very valuable from me, and I'm going to get it back.
- What did he steal from you? -Atlan wanted to know.
- "That's none of your business," said The Ninja. Just stay away from here, or you'll regret it.

Atlan couldn't believe what he heard. The Ninja was ungrateful and selfish. He didn't care about anything but his revenge.

- "I'm not going to leave," Atlan said. I'm not going to let you kill that man.
- That? -The Ninja was surprised-. How do you know what I'm going to do?

- "I know because I've seen it on the news," Atlan said. You're a murderer, just like him.
- "I'm not a murderer, I'm a vigilante," said The Ninja. I do what the law does not do. I eliminate criminals who get away with it.
- "That is not justice, it is violence," said Atlan. You can't take anyone's life, no matter how bad it is.
- And what do you know about life? -The Ninja asked-. You're just a kid playing hero. You know nothing about pain, suffering, loss.
- "Maybe not, but I know what is right and what is wrong," Atlan said. And you are very wrong.

The two looked at each other defiantly, as Lepidum recovered from his attack. The villain took advantage of his rivals' distraction to fire another beam of red ions, this time aimed at both of them.

Atlan and The Ninja reacted at the same time, jumping in opposite directions to avoid the impact. However, the beam was so powerful that it caused an explosion when it collided with the ground, causing a shock wave that launched them into the air.

Atlan fell on a pile of scrap metal, while The Ninja fell on the roof of a car. Both were knocked unconscious by the blow.

Lepidum watched them with an evil smile.

- Ha, ha, ha - laughed Lepidum -. Pathetic. Neither of them is a match for me. Now I will finish you both off, and then I will leave with my loot.

Lepidum slowly approached his fallen enemies, ready to deliver the final blow. However, before he could do so, a voice stopped him.

- "Stop there, Lepidum," said the voice. Your days of evil are over.

Lepidum turned and saw a group of police officers armed with guns and shields. Among them was Commissioner Pérez, the head of the local police.

- "Damn," Lepidum muttered. Police.
- Yes, the police - said Commissioner Pérez -. We have followed your trail here. We know that you are responsible for the theft of the nuclear reactor from the secret laboratory. We order you to surrender and hand over the reactor to us.

-

Lepidum looked at the briefcase in his hand. Inside was the nuclear reactor that he had stolen from the secret laboratory.

It was a very powerful and very dangerous source of energy.

Lepidum planned to use it to create a bomb capable of destroying the entire city...

Lepidum had stolen a nuclear reactor from the secret laboratory of the Medical Union...

The Ninja had followed Lepidum to the factory, since the nuclear reactor was something very valuable to him for personal reasons.

Atlan had arrived later, feeling a vibration in his spider sense that warned him of danger.

Atlan and The Ninja had faced Lepidum with their different abilities and weapons, but the villain had surpassed them with his metallic moth suit, which allowed him to fly and shoot high-intensity red ions.
Lepidum had wounded both with his lightning, leaving them weakened.

Lepidum had approached them to finish them off, but before he could do so, he had been surprised by the arrival of the police.
Commissioner Pérez, the local police chief, had ordered him to surrender and hand over the nuclear reactor.

Lepidum had refused to do so, and had activated the nuclear reactor and launched it into the air.

He had then fired a beam of red ions into the reactor, causing a chain reaction that led to a massive nuclear explosion.

The explosion had illuminated the night sky in a blinding white glow. A mushroom cloud had risen over the city, while radioactive fallout fell on it.

Lepidum and the police officers had been instantly vaporized by the explosion.

Atlan and The Ninja had been hit by the blast wave, but had survived thanks to their protective suits.

That's what happened minutes before the bomb detonated. It was a terrible and tragic moment, which changed the lives of everyone who lived in the city.

Atlan was horrified by what had happened. He couldn't believe that Lepidum had been able to do something so terrible. He had destroyed the city and killed thousands of people, including the police officers who had tried to arrest him.

Atlan stood up with difficulty and looked around. Everything was in ruins.

Smoke and fire covered the landscape. Buildings were collapsed, cars smashed, bodies scattered. There were no signs of life.

Atlan wondered if there were any survivors. Maybe his family, his friends, his neighbors. Maybe they could have escaped or taken refuge somewhere safe.

Atlan hoped that would be the case, but he doubted it.
Atlan felt alone and desperate. He didn't know what to do or where to go.
He felt guilty for not having been able to prevent the catastrophe. He wondered if he could have done anything differently, if he could have convinced The Ninja to join him, if he could have defeated Lepidum before he activated the reactor.

Atlan realized that there was no point in regretting the past.

What was done was done. The only thing she could do was keep going and try to find a way to survive and help others.

Atlan remembered that he had a communicator in his suit, which allowed him to contact other heroes or the authorities. Maybe someone would have answered his call for help.

Atlan took out the communicator and activated it.

- "This is Atlan, the spider hero," he said. Anyone there? Does anyone listen to me?

Atlan waited a few seconds, but there was no response. All you could hear was static.

- "Please respond," Atlan insisted. I need help. The city has been attacked by Lepidum, the moth villain. He has detonated a nuclear reactor and caused a massive explosion. I don't know if there are survivors. I am alone and hurt.

Atlan waited again, but no one answered. The communicator was broken or no one had survived the attack.

Atlan felt even more alone and desperate. He wondered if there was any point in continuing to live.

Suddenly, he heard a faint moan near him.

It was The Ninja, who had also survived the explosion thanks to his protective suit.

The Ninja was lying on the roof of a car, with several bleeding wounds and burns on his body.

His red hood was torn and his black mask was torn, revealing part of his face.

Atlan recognized him instantly. It was a boy a little older than him, about sixteen years old, with amethyst hair and purple eyes.

Atlan had seen him before at school, where he was one of the most popular and rebellious students.

His name was Zhen Jun, and he was the son of the Director of the Global Medical Union...

Atlan approached him cautiously, not knowing if he was friend or foe.

- Hello, Atlan said. Are you OK?

The Ninja opened his eyes and saw Atlan in front of him.

- "You..." The Ninja murmured. You are the weirdo...

- "Yes, it's me," said Atlan. I am Atlan, the spider hero.

- What do you want? -The Ninja asked-.

- Are you coming to finish me off?

- "No, I'm not here to finish you off," Atlan said. I come to help you.

- Help me? -The Ninja repeated-. Because?

- Because we are the only ones left -said Atlan-. Lepidum has killed everyone else. He has exploded a nuclear reactor and devastated the city.

The Ninja remained silent, processing the information.

- A nuclear reactor? -The Ninja asked-. Was that what he stole from me?

- "Yes, that was what he stole from you," Atlan confirmed. What were you doing with a nuclear reactor?

- "That's none of your business," said The Ninja. It was something personal.

- "Well, whatever it is, it doesn't matter anymore," said Atlan. The only thing that matters now is survival.

- Survive? -The Ninja asked-. So that? What's the point of living in this hell?

- "It makes sense if we help each other," Atlan said. If we unite and look for a way out. If we find other survivors and help them. If we rebuild the city and make it better.

- Better? -The Ninja asked-. How is it going to be better? This city was rotten before. Full of corruption, violence, injustice. Full of people like Lepidum, who just wanted to destroy everything.
- "Not everyone was like that," Atlan said. There were good people, people who deserved to live. People like my family, my friends, my neighbors. People like you.

- Like me? -The Ninja asked-. Don't compare me to them. I am not good. I am an antihero, a vigilante, a murderer.

- "You are not a murderer," Atlan said. You are a hero, even if you don't know it. You have fought evil, you have helped people, you have saved lives.

- "I have also taken lives," said The Ninja. I have killed many criminals, without mercy or remorse. I have done what the law did not do. I have taken justice into my own hands.

- **"That is not justice, it is violence," said Atlan. You can't take anyone's life, no matter how bad it is.**

- **And what do you know about life? -The Ninja asked-. You're just a kid playing hero. You know nothing about pain, suffering, loss.**

- **"Maybe not, but I know what is right and what is wrong," Atlan said. And you are very wrong.**

The two looked at each other with defiance, but also with curiosity. They realized that they had a lot in common, but also many differences. They realized they needed each other, but they also feared each other.

Atlan extended his hand towards The Ninja, offering his help.

- **"Come on," Atlan said. We can't stay here. We have to find a way out. We have to look for hope.**

The Ninja looked at Atlan's hand, hesitating whether to accept it or reject it.

- Why should I trust you? -The Ninja asked-. Why should I follow you?

- Because we are the only ones left, Atlan repeated. Because we are the only ones who can do something. Because we are the only ones who can change things.

The Ninja thought about Atlan's words. He thought about what had happened. He thought about what he wanted to do.

Finally, he took Atlan's hand and stood up with his help.

- "It's okay," said The Ninja. I will follow you. But don't expect me to change my way of being. Don't expect me to become a hero like you.

- "I'm not asking you to change," Atlan said. I just ask you to give me a chance. An opportunity to show you that there is another way of doing things. A better way.

The two smiled knowingly and set off. Together they faced the dangers and obstacles that awaited them in the devastated city. Together they looked for a way out and hope. Together they started a new adventure...

End, for now?

More from the author:

Caves and Diamonds: a Kairos adventure

Luna and Rex: A Space Odyssey

Solomon's clavicles

The Emerald Tablet: Art Book

Bones' diary

The Oracle of Lourdes

Drawing Manual: aptitude for your drawings

Drawing Manual: dynamic line

Drawing Manual: meme special

Drawing Manual: natural elements